Eleanor Roosevelt
First Lady & Equal Rights Advocate

by Grace Hansen

Abdo
HISTORY MAKER BIOGRAPHIES
Kids

abdopublishing.com

Published by Abdo Kids, a division of ABDO, PO Box 398166, Minneapolis, Minnesota 55439.

Copyright © 2016 by Abdo Consulting Group, Inc. International copyrights reserved in all countries. No part of this book may be reproduced in any form without written permission from the publisher.

Printed in the United States of America, North Mankato, Minnesota.

102015

012016

 THIS BOOK CONTAINS RECYCLED MATERIALS

Photo Credits: AP Images, Corbis, Getty Images, iStock, Shutterstock

Production Contributors: Teddy Borth, Jennie Forsberg, Grace Hansen

Design Contributors: Laura Mitchell, Dorothy Toth

Library of Congress Control Number: 2015941772

Cataloging-in-Publication Data

Hansen, Grace.

 Eleanor Roosevelt: First Lady & equal rights advocate / Grace Hansen.

  p. cm. -- (History maker biographies)

Includes index.

ISBN 978-1-68080-123-1

1. Roosevelt, Eleanor, 1884-1962--Juvenile literature. 2. Presidents' spouses--United States--Biography--Juvenile literature. 1. Title.

973.917/092--dc23

[B]

2015941772

Table of Contents

Early Life 4

Making a Difference 12

Death & Legacy 20

Timeline. 22

Glossary 23

Index 24

Abdo Kids Code. 24

Early Life

Anna Eleanor Roosevelt

was born on October 11, 1884.

She grew up in New York City,

New York.

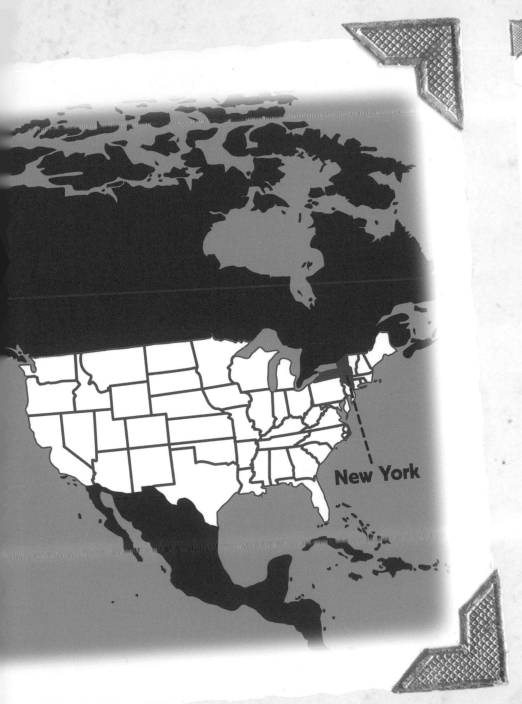

New York

Eleanor was a shy child. She did not feel important. She left for England at age 15. She went to boarding school. There, she became a strong person.

7

Eleanor returned home ready to make a difference. She started work at a **settlement house**. She taught **immigrant** children.

In 1902, Eleanor met Franklin Roosevelt. They married on March 17, 1905. They had six children.

11

Making a Difference

In 1933, Franklin became the 32nd president. This made Eleanor the **First Lady**. She used her title to help many people.

Franklin had been sick for many years. Traveling was hard for him. So Eleanor often traveled for him. She met people all over the country. She learned about their problems.

15

Eleanor knew what it was like to feel weak. So she spoke for people who were treated unfairly. She helped American workers and the poor. She helped women and African Americans.

In 1946, Eleanor was elected to the **United Nations**. Her focus was on human rights. Now she could help people around the world.

19

Death & Legacy

Eleanor forever changed the role of the **First Lady**. She worked to do what was right and good. She died on November 7, 1962.

Timeline

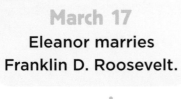

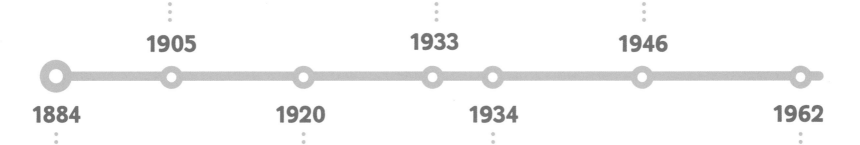

March 17
Eleanor marries Franklin D. Roosevelt.

Eleanor becomes the **First Lady** of the United States.

Eleanor is elected to the **United Nations** as the head of the Human Rights Commission.

1905

1933

1946

1884

1920

1934

1962

October 11
Anna Eleanor Roosevelt is born in New York City, New York.

Eleanor joins the League of Women Voters. Women get the right to vote later that year.

Eleanor begins work with the **NAACP** to help in the fight for equality.

November 7
Eleanor dies at the age of 78.

Glossary

First Lady – the wife of the chief executive of a country.

immigrant – a person who moves from one country to another to live.

NAACP – stands for the National Association for the Advancement of Colored People. The organization formed in 1909 to ensure equality of rights of all persons, and to end racism.

settlement house – a place that provides community services to people in a crowded part of a city.

United Nations – a group made up of most of the world's countries. It was created in 1945 to promote peace, security, and unity.

Index

African Americans 16, 18

birth 4

children 10

death 20

First Lady 12, 20

human rights 18

New York 4

Roosevelt, Franklin 10, 12, 14

school 6

United Nations 18

women 16

work 8, 14, 16, 18

abdokids.com

Use this code to log on to abdokids.com and access crafts, games, videos, and more!

Abdo Kids Code:
HEK1231